Electing the President

Revised Edition

Revised Edition

For Grades 4–8

★ Electing the President

President

An Interactive Simulation on the Electoral Process

Betty M. See

Routledge
Taylor & Francis Group

NEW YORK AND LONDON

First published in 2012 by Prufrock Press Inc.

Published in 2021 by Routledge
605 Third Avenue, New York, NY 10017
2 Park Square, Milton Park, Abingdon, Oxon OX14 4RN

Routledge is an imprint of the Taylor & Francis Group, an informa business.

Copyright © 2012 by Taylor & Francis Group.

Production design by Raquel Trevino

ISBN-13: 978-1-5936-3993-8 (pbk)

DOI: 10.4324/9781003234869

Contents

Information for the Instructor

Forms and Handouts for Students

Student Guides

Introduction and Overview

Why Do This?

"Why do we have to do this?" This may be a question your students ask you or perhaps a question you even ask yourself. Why take 7 days out of your teaching year to conduct a simulation about how the leaders of our country are chosen? The reason is that it is important for students to understand how the election process works, how a process that was put in place more than 200 years ago has survived, and what happens to their individual votes.

Forget the fact that learning by doing means that students will remember the lessons long after they leave your class. Forget the fact that simulations are motivating and often draw out the more reticent learners in your classroom. You need to do this because it is important. The success of a democracy is dependent on an educated populace. This implies not only that the citizens can read and write but also that they are knowledgeable about how the government works and also about their rights and responsibilities. Voting is both a right and a responsibility. It is important that all citizens feel that they are a part of the process and that their votes count.

The Concept

The election of a President and Vice President of the United States is unique in that the candidates who receive most of the votes by the citizens (called the popular vote) may not necessarily be the winners. The voters are actually voting for a slate of electors when they cast their ballot every 4 years for the President and Vice President. The candidates who receive the most popular votes in each state will receive all of the electoral votes for that state—a winner-take-all method (the only two states that do not follow this traditional method are Maine and Nebraska). This concept can be difficult for students to understand and to remember.

By holding a simulated presidential election, the students will understand our Electoral College system, and they will become aware of the many steps involved in electing a President and Vice President. This simulation will allow

DOI: 10.4324/9781003234869-1

you to conduct an election on several different levels, depending on your classroom situation and the number of students involved. By actually taking part in the process, students will experience the electoral process firsthand and will see how important it is to vote.

Overview

This simulation works well with one class, several classes, or a larger student population of students in grades 4–8. It has been conducted successfully with as few as 15 students and as many as 450. Upon completing the simulation, the students should have a good understanding of our country's multiparty system, the purpose of political conventions, voter registration, campaigning, and the Electoral College. During the simulation, all students will become actively involved and should be well on their way to becoming more informed voters as adults.

Most of this book consists of instructions for the teacher that spell out the procedures for conducting the simulation. This includes:
- ✓ an overview and historical background that you can share orally with your students,
- ✓ instructions for staging the simulation,
- ✓ several forms that will be used in the simulation, and
- ✓ a copy of the parts of the U.S. Constitution that govern the election of the President and Vice President.

Your Role

Prior to beginning the simulation, you will need to give students background information about the election process. If this simulation is being used in conjunction with a unit on the Constitution or a unit on the political process, students will already have some basic knowledge about the electoral process. If not, you will have to provide an overview of the way our leaders are elected. This information is included for you on pages 3–7 and handouts for students are provided on pages 39–45.

During the simulation, you must remain an unbiased observer and consultant. Your role is to provide the guidelines and see that they are followed—but let the students do the work and experience the election process firsthand.

Background Information

Democracy

A *democracy* is a system of government that gives citizens the right to influence political decisions either directly or indirectly. Direct democracy (where citizens as a whole are responsible for making decisions) is possible only when the population is small. The United States has what is called a representative democracy. This means that although citizens are given the right to vote on issues and leaders, many of the decisions are not made by direct popular vote, but are decided instead by elected representatives.

Elections are an important element of a democracy. They reinforce the government's authority and serve as a communication between the voters and the politicians. This ensures that the government responds to the wishes of the majority of its citizens. In some countries, voting is compulsory; in other countries, voting is not mandatory, but voter registration is automatic. In the United States, both registration and voting are voluntary; as a result, we have a much lower voter turnout than other countries.

In electoral systems, there are two ways of converting the citizens' votes to actual election of office holders. One is the majoritarian system in which the candidate who receives the plurality of votes by getting at least 50% (or some other measure) wins. The other system is the proportional system by which the distribution of seats is proportional to the number of votes cast. The selection of electors, and hence the selection of the President and Vice President in the United States, is by the majoritarian system in all but two states (Maine and Nebraska).

Primaries

Holding primary elections and caucuses would be quite complicated and time-consuming and, therefore, it is not practical to include them during this simulation given the time constraints of the classroom. However, students should be aware of how the system works. You might want to explain primary elections and caucuses in the following way.

DOI: 10.4324/9781003234869-2

Most states hold primary elections or caucuses on various dates throughout the first half of an election year (January through June) in which people vote for a candidate. It is important to know that the votes cast during the primary elections and caucuses could actually be considered an indirect vote, as delegates are granted to each state and it is these delegates who will eventually go on to their party's national convention and cast a vote for the presidential nominee.

Candidates begin their campaigning early in the year. Because the primary elections and caucuses are held on different dates, the candidates usually concentrate their campaigns on states whose election dates are the nearest. There may be many candidates early in the campaign, but candidates who do not do well in the early primaries usually drop out. As a result, by the time primary elections are held in some states in May or June, the field may be narrowed to only one or two candidates for each party.

Conventions

After all of the primary elections and caucuses, each party holds a convention in the summer in which delegates from each state select a presidential candidate and decide on a platform. The platform is a body of principles or issues on which the party takes a stand. The selection of the presidential candidate is usually the most exciting and visible aspect of the convention. After the presidential candidate is selected, he or she selects a running mate (the vice presidential candidate). The procedure of deciding on a platform is not as visible and usually involves negotiations between party leaders and the party's two candidates.

When the political conventions are held in the summer, the delegates vote on the first ballot for the candidate who won the state's primary election (although there is no law enforcing that delegates vote for the person who won the state's primary, delegates rarely change their vote). If there is no candidate who receives a majority of the votes on the first ballot, additional ballots are held until one candidate has a majority of the votes. After the first ballot, each delegate is free to vote for the candidate of his or her choice.

The Democratic and Republican parties have a fairly complex method for allocating convention delegates to each state. They are distributed according to state population, but other factors, such as electoral votes won by a state during the previous presidential election, may be considered. Because this method would be too difficult to implement in your classroom simulation, it is best to have one vote per student. Should you care to find out how the Democratic and Republican parties determine how many delegates each state will have, you can access their websites (http://www.democrats.org and http://www.gop.com) to find detailed information.

Elector Selection

Article II, Section 1 of the United States Constitution deals with the election of the President and the Vice President (see the Appendix for a copy of both Article II and the Twelfth Amendment, which discusses the procedure for electing the President and Vice President). The number of electors each state has is determined by the number of members that state has in the House of Representatives, plus the two Senators each state has. Because the representation in the House is based on population, those states with the largest populations will have the most electors. There are 538 votes in all (435 Representatives, 100 Senators, and 3 electors from the District of Columbia). Typically, the political parties nominate their lists of electors at their respective state conventions. The states may choose to list these electors on the ballot or may only list the candidates for President and Vice President.

Popular Vote

The presidential election is held the first Tuesday after the first Monday in November every fourth year. In each state, the candidate receiving the most popular votes for that state wins all of the electoral votes (except for Maine and Nebraska) and the losing candidates get no electors. When someone votes for a candidate, he or she is really voting for an elector who will vote for that candidate. In some states, electors are required to vote for their party's candidate, but in other states they may vote for candidates from other parties (although that rarely happens). The two exceptions to the winner-take-all method are Maine and Nebraska, where two electors are chosen by statewide popular vote and the remaining electors are chosen by popular vote within each Congressional district.

Electoral College Vote

The electors representing the party whose candidate received the most popular votes meet on the first Monday after the second Wednesday in December in their respective state capitals. These electors cannot be members of Congress or hold any federal office. They vote for their candidates, and these votes are then sealed and sent to the president of the United States Senate. On January 6, at a joint meeting of the House of Representatives and the Senate, the ballots are opened and officially counted. A majority of the 538, or 270 electoral votes, is needed for a candidate to be declared a winner. The Twelfth Amendment of the Constitution gives the procedure for electing a President if no one candidate receives a majority.

History

When it was written into the Constitution, the use of electors was a compromise between using a direct popular vote and choosing leaders by inheritance or appointment. It was also seen as a way to share power between the states and the national government. In the early years of the Electoral College, several states let their legislators choose the electors. By 1828, all states except South Carolina gave voters the ability to vote for the electors and then let the winning party's electors cast the state's votes for the presidential candidate. There is no law that requires the electors to vote for the party they represent but it is rare that electors would cast a vote for someone other than their party's candidate.

Before the adoption of the Twelfth Amendment, the electors voted for two persons, and the person with the majority won the office of President and the runner-up became Vice President. In 1796, John Adams and Thomas Jefferson finished first and second, making Adams the President and Jefferson the Vice President even though they were fierce foes. In 1800, Thomas Jefferson and Aaron Burr, both nominees of the Democratic Republican party, received exactly the same number of votes. Although Jefferson was his party's candidate for President, it took the House of Representatives 36 ballots before Jefferson was elected. These problems led to the adoption of the Twelfth Amendment, which required that electors cast separate ballots for President and Vice President.

The total number of electoral votes has changed as our population and number of states have increased. In 1789, the first House of Representatives had 65 members. In 1910, the number of representatives was fixed at 435. As states were added, the number of senators (with two per state) increased to the present number of 100. With the District of Columbia's three electors, this makes a total of 538 electors.

Three Exceptions

Even after the passage of the Twelfth Amendment in 1804, the method of electing a President by the Electoral College has not been without its problems. Because the President is not chosen by popular vote, but is instead chosen by the electoral vote totals, it is possible that the candidate who wins the popular vote does not get enough electoral votes to win the election. There have been three instances when the candidates receiving the most popular votes were not elected President.

1876	Popular Votes	Electoral Votes
Samuel J. Tilden	4,284,020	184
Rutherford B. Hayes	4,036,572	185
Total electoral votes: 369		

1888	Popular Votes	Electoral Votes
Benjamin Harrison	5,443,892	233
Grover Cleveland	5,534,488	168

Total electoral votes: 401

Had Grover Cleveland won this election, he would have served three consecutive terms, for he defeated Benjamin Harrison in 1892 by more than 300,000 popular votes and 132 electoral votes.

2000	Popular Votes	Electoral Votes
George W. Bush	50,456,002	271
Albert Gore	50,999,897	266*

Total electoral votes: 537

* Gore lost an electoral vote because one District of Columbia elector left her ballot blank to protest the District's lack of voting power in Congress.

There have been many people who have argued that the use of the Electoral College to determine the presidency is unfair. This procedure has not been changed, however, because legislators are reluctant to change any part of the Constitution that has served Americans so well for so long.

Eligibility Rules

Article II, Section 1 of the Constitution also lists the eligibility requirements for an individual to become President. Because the Vice President assumes leadership if the President can no longer continue in office, these rules also apply to the Vice President. Candidates must be:
- ✓ natural-born citizens of the United States,
- ✓ at least 35 years old, and
- ✓ residents of the United States for at least 14 years.

In addition, the presidential and vice presidential candidates for each party should be from different states. The Twelfth Amendment states that if the two candidates are from the same state, electors from that state can vote for only one of the candidates and have to cast their other vote for a candidate from another state. Not wanting to throw away a potential elector vote, parties will usually look for a vice presidential candidate who resides in a different state than the presidential candidate.

Before You Start

Electors

Look up the current apportionment of electors. Because the apportionment changes with each census, you will need to access a current reference to get an accurate count for each state. You can find an up-to-date apportionment on the U.S. Census Bureau's website or you can contact your Senators or Representatives. The census is taken every 10 years, so information gathered in the 2010 census will affect all elections until the census in 2020. The information in this book is based on the 2010 census.

Overview

It is imperative that the students understand the entire election process. They must see the whole picture before they begin the preliminary activities. This simulation works best if they already have some knowledge of the Constitution and the historical background of our presidential elections. If they have not previously studied this, present the brief overview provided on pages 39–45. In particular, discuss the Electoral College and how the votes are apportioned to each state.

Divide the Class

Decide how many students will be involved in the simulation. Divide this group into two political parties. You may do this randomly, or you may wish to form the two groups so they are balanced, in that each group has a few students who are outgoing enough and meet the qualifications to be candidates. These parties will each select presidential and vice presidential candidates at their conventions.

Eligibility Rules

Early in the simulation, you will want to explain to the students that there are certain eligibility rules if someone wishes to become President or Vice President of the United States. Tell them that there will be special rules for

DOI: 10.4324/9781003234869-3

the purpose of your classroom election. Before you begin the simulation, you should establish rules that you feel are appropriate to your student population. For instance, you may wish to waive the "natural-born citizen of the United States" requirement and shorten the length of residency. A set of rules might include the following:

- ✓ A candidate must be at least _____ years old.
- ✓ A candidate must have been a resident of our town for at least _____ months.

You can add other qualifications as you find necessary, but the qualifications should not be too restrictive.

Campaign Rules

On Day 4 of the simulation, your class will have to establish rules for campaigning. It will help if you give this issue some thought before you bring it up to the students. You need to give students some guidance about what practices are realistic and acceptable. You might want to:

- ✓ designate times and places where campaigning may take place,
- ✓ specify poster size and places where they may be displayed, and
- ✓ discourage the distribution of items such as candy or pencils, as this gives an unfair advantage to students who have the means to provide them.

Platforms

You should prepare a list of issues that you feel are appropriate for the age and sophistication of your students. You can use the Election Issues handout (pp. 27–30) as a starting point. If students propose other issues, it is a good opportunity to discuss what issues fall under the domain of the federal government and what issues are handled primarily by state and local governments. On many issues, there may not be clear-cut divisions between the role of the federal government and other jurisdictions, as many roles overlap or are influenced by the policies of the higher levels of government.

Ask students to decide which issues are the most significant in this election and to take positions on these issues. In addition to the issues outlined on pages 27–30, some other issues to consider are:

- ✓ foreign policy;
- ✓ export/import policies and tariffs on foreign goods;
- ✓ social programs such as welfare, job training, and mental health;
- ✓ campaign finance reform;

✓ space exploration;
✓ funding for the humanities and arts; and
✓ funding for science.

Apportion Votes

One of the more important things you will do is decide how to divide up the states' electoral votes among the students. Because this can be time-consuming, it is advised that you do it prior to beginning the simulation. Detailed instructions and examples are provided to guide you through this process.

Read through the detailed information on pages 13–20, and decide how you will divide the electoral votes. Divide the states so that each voter has approximately the same number of electoral votes.

Make Electoral Assignments

Duplicate the Assignment of Electoral College Vote form on page 33. Record the states that will be represented by each voter on the bottom portion of the form as well as the electoral votes for each state. Write the student's name at the top. Distribute the assignments on Day 4 of the simulation. Remember that in most cases, students will play two roles: voters in the popular election and members of the Electoral College.

Prepare Ballots

Prior to voting on Day 6, the ballots for the electoral vote (p. 35) should be duplicated and prepared. One ballot should be prepared for each state, noting how many electoral votes that state has.

In the case where one voting bloc (whether it is one student or several students) has been assigned only one state (such as California), the bloc will receive only one electoral ballot, listing that one state. If more than one student is in the voting bloc, they each will cast a popular vote using their popular vote ballots. After casting their popular votes, the candidate who receives the majority of votes in that voting bloc will be recorded on the electoral vote ballot.

In the case of a voting bloc (either one student or a group of students) that has been assigned several states, the bloc will receive a ballot for each state. These ballots should be stapled together and labeled with the student's name or the number of the voting bloc (e.g., Voting Bloc 39). If one person is representing several states, he or she must vote for the same candidate for all of the

assigned states. If there are several people in the voting bloc, each person will vote for the candidates separately (this is the popular vote using the popular vote ballots), but once the voters have indicated their popular vote, the winning candidate (the one with the most popular votes) will be recorded on *all* electoral ballots (this is the electoral vote). See pages 17–18 for examples.

In the case of multiple classes, each class should be divided into groups of voters, with each group representing one or several states. When the voters in each group vote (the popular vote using the popular vote ballots), the majority will determine the candidate who will get all of their states' electoral votes. Three people, then, may vote individually (popular vote), but as a group, they will submit only one electoral ballot for the candidate who received the majority of their votes for each state they represent. In the example on page 19, Class 3 will cast 19 individual votes on popular ballots and will then submit electoral ballots for the seven states they represent. The class will have a total of 47 electoral votes for these seven states.

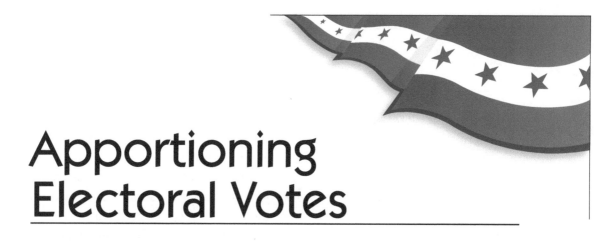

Apportioning Electoral Votes

The Procedure

One of the first things you will need to do before you begin the simulation is to decide how to apportion the electoral votes. Depending on the number of students in your group, you may have one student represent several states or, in the case of larger groups, you may have several students represent one large state with many electors.

To determine the number of electoral votes each student represents, divide 538 (the total number of electoral votes) by the number of students involved in the simulation. Once you have calculated approximately how many electoral votes each student in the simulation should represent, you must decide how you will divide up the states and their electoral votes so that each student has roughly the same number of votes. To do this, refer to the map on page 31 that shows how many electors each state is allocated. Begin grouping states so that the total number of electors for any one group or individual is around the number you have calculated to be the appropriate number for each of your students.

For instance, if you have 15 students, you would divide 538 by 15 and get 35.86, which is approximately 36. You would then look at the list of states and their electors and try to group them so that the total of each grouping is about 36. The Sample Distribution of Electoral Votes shown on pages 15–16 shows one example of how this could be done.

If you have 46 students, each student would get approximately 12 electoral votes. If Texas has three students representing its 38 votes, they would each cast a vote (this is the popular vote). Whichever candidate got the majority of the three votes would get all of the electoral votes. Prior to the election, the three students representing the Texas voting bloc will be given an electoral ballot with Texas and its electoral votes listed on the ballot. When the popular votes are tallied, the candidate receiving the most votes will receive all of the state's electoral votes. The result is recorded on the electoral vote ballot.

If you have a small group of students, you may not be able to maintain a balanced ratio. In this case, try to group the states as evenly as possible and assign them randomly or have students draw for them.

 DOI: 10.4324/9781003234869-4

Let students know before Election Day which states they will represent. On Election Day, distribute ballots with individual state names and corresponding electoral votes to the students representing these states.

A word of caution: If you have an even number of students representing one state, determine beforehand how you will break a tie should they not be able to agree on a candidate. One possible solution would be to draw a candidate's name from a hat. The name drawn would receive all of the electoral votes. Be sure a tie is broken before final tallies are made so that students are not influenced by the possible outcome.

Example: Smaller Groups

If you have a group of 46 students participating in the simulation, you would divide 538 by 46:

538 ÷ 46 students = 11.70, or an average of 12 electoral votes per student

Using this as a rule of thumb, you may assign one student any of the states having between 10 and 15 electoral votes (e.g., Massachusetts, which currently has 11 votes). You might also assign this student one or more states whose total electoral votes are between 10 and 15 (e.g., Iowa, which currently has 6 votes, and Kansas, which currently has 6 votes). For states with a larger number of electoral votes, you may assign more than one student. For instance, Texas (38 votes) might have three students assigned to it.

In the case where one student represents several states, her one vote translates into electoral votes for her selected candidate for *all* of the states represented. For example, if a student is representing both Iowa and Kansas, one popular vote for the Do Right candidate gives 12 electoral votes to this candidate.

Example: Multiple Classes

If you are conducting the simulation with multiple classes, using the same formula, divide the number of electoral votes (538) by the number of students involved. For example, if you have 240 students, you would divide 538 by 240:

538 ÷ 240 = 2.24, or an average of 2 electoral votes per student

Using this as a guideline, assign each classroom one or more states. Classrooms with a larger number of students would be assigned states such as California (55 votes), New York (29 votes), or Texas (38 votes). Try to apportion the states among the classes as equitably as possible to keep the ratio of students to electoral votes fairly even; however, try to have an odd number of students representing each state to avoid the problems a tie might cause. Some classes may represent several smaller states. In fact, one student may represent a state such as Montana, which has only 3 electoral votes.

In the case of a simulation that involves several classes, each one will be assigned several states and groups of students will be assigned to each state. When the students assigned to a state (e.g., Ohio) vote, the candidate who receives the majority of the votes gets all 18 of Ohio's electoral votes. Other students in the class will be assigned to different states, and their votes are allocated to the winning candidate in the same manner.

Sample Distribution of Electoral Votes

Below is an example of how one teacher divided the electoral votes. This example is based on a class of 15 students. In the distribution, you would try to come as close to 36 votes for each elector as possible (538 ÷ 15 ≈ 36), although some students will have more and some will have less. There are, of course various ways to divide up the votes and still have a fair distribution. The chart below shows one way that this can be done.

Example Electoral Distribution for 15 Students

Voter 1	Voter 2	Voter 3
California: 55 Total: **55**	Texas: 38 New Mexico: 5 Arizona: 11 Total: **54**	Florida: 29 Georgia: 16 South Carolina: 9 Total: **54**
Voter 4	**Voter 5**	**Voter 6**
Illinois: 20 Missouri: 10 Nebraska: 5 Kansas: 6 South Dakota: 3 Total: **44**	Louisiana: 8 Arkansas: 6 Oklahoma: 7 Alabama: 9 Mississippi: 6 Total: **36**	Ohio: 18 Kentucky: 8 Tennessee: 11 Total: **37**

Voter 7	Voter 8	Voter 9
Michigan: 16 Indiana: 11 Total: **27**	Pennsylvania: 20 West Virginia: 5 Total: **25**	North Dakota: 3 Wisconsin: 10 Minnesota: 10 Iowa: 6 Total: **29**
Voter 10	**Voter 11**	**Voter 12**
Utah: 6 Nevada: 6 Montana: 3 Wyoming: 3 Colorado: 9 Total: **27**	Massachusetts: 11 Maine: 4 New Hampshire: 4 Vermont: 3 Rhode Island: 4 Connecticut: 7 Total: **33**	Washington: 12 Oregon: 7 Idaho: 4 Alaska: 3 Hawaii: 4 Total: **30**
Voter 13	**Voter 14**	**Voter 15**
Virginia: 13 North Carolina: 15 Total: **28**	New Jersey: 14 Delaware: 3 Maryland: 10 District of Columbia: 3 Total: **30**	New York: 29 Total: **29**

There are a total of 538. In this case, it is possible for a candidate to win the popular vote from the first six voters, thereby receiving 280 electoral votes and winning the election.

Sample distributions for 15, 46, and 240 students are included on the pages that follow.

Sample Distribution of Electoral Votes: 15 Students

Below is a random selection of votes per student for a group of 15 students. Students should be given approximately 36 votes each, but the range in this example is 25–55 votes per student. In this example, the Fair and Square Party wins the election with 280 electoral votes.

	EV	Fair and Square Party		Do Right Party	
		EV	PV	EV	PV
Voter 1					
California	55	55	1		
Total	**55**	**55**	1		
Voter 2					
Texas	38	38			
New Mexico	5	5			
Arizona	11	11			
Total	**54**	**54**	1		
Voter 3					
Florida	29	29			
Georgia	16	16			
South Carolina	9	9			
Total	**54**	**54**	1		
Voter 4					
Illinois	20	20			
Missouri	10	10			
Nebraska	5	5			
Kansas	6	6			
South Dakota	3	3			
Total	**44**	**44**	1		
Voter 5					
Louisiana	8	8			
Arkansas	6	6			
Oklahoma	7	7			
Alabama	9	9			
Mississippi	6	6			
Total	**36**	**36**	1		

	EV	Fair and Square Party		Do Right Party	
		EV	PV	EV	PV
Voter 6					
Ohio	18	18			
Kentucky	8	8			
Tennessee	11	11			
Total	**37**	**37**	1		
Voter 7					
Michigan	16			16	
Indiana	11			11	
Total	**27**			**27**	1
Voter 8					
Pennsylvania	20			20	
West Virginia	5			5	
Total	**25**			**25**	1
Voter 9					
North Dakota	3			3	
Wisconsin	10			10	
Minnesota	10			10	
Iowa	6			6	
Total	**29**			**29**	1
Voter 10					
Utah	6			6	
Nevada	6			6	
Montana	3			3	
Wyoming	3			3	
Colorado	9			9	
Total	**27**			**27**	1

	EV	Fair and Square Party		Do Right Party	
		EV	PV	EV	PV
Voter 11					
Massachusetts	11			11	
Maine	4			4	
New Hampshire	4			4	
Vermont	3			3	
Rhode Island	4			4	
Connecticut	7			7	
Total	**33**			**33**	1
Voter 12					
Washington	12			12	
Oregon	7			7	
Idaho	4			4	
Alaska	3			3	
Hawaii	4			4	
Total	**30**			**30**	1
Voter 13					
Virginia	13			13	
North Carolina	15			15	
Total	**28**			**28**	1
Voter 14					
New Jersey	14			14	
Delaware	3			3	
Maryland	10			10	
District of Columbia	3			3	
Total	**30**			**30**	1
Voter 15					
New York	29			29	
Total	**29**			**29**	1
Grand Totals	**538**	**280**	**6**	**258**	**9**

EV = electoral vote; PV = popular vote

Sample Distribution of Electoral Votes: 46 Students

Below is a random selection of votes per student for a group of 46 students. Students should be given approximately 12 votes each, but the range in this example is approximately 9–15 votes per student. In this example, the Do Right Party wins the election with 278 electoral votes.

	EV	Fair and Square Party		Do Right Party	
		EV	PV	EV	PV
Voters 1–5 (5)			3		2
California	55	55			
Voters 6–8 (3)			2		1
Florida	29	29			
Rhode Island	4	4			
Voters 9–11 (3)			1		2
Illinois	20			20	
Nevada	6			6	
South Dakota	3			3	
Voters 12–14 (3)			1		2
New York	29			29	
New Hampshire	4			4	
Voters 15–17 (3)			1		2
Texas	38			38	
Voters 18–20 (3)			1		2
Ohio	18			18	
Colorado	9			9	
Delaware	3			3	
Voters 21–23 (3)			1		2
Pennsylvania	20			20	
Michigan	16			16	
Voter 24 (1)			1		
North Dakota	3	3			
South Carolina	9	9			
Voter 25 (1)			1		
North Carolina	15	15			
Voter 26 (1)			1		
New Jersey	14	14			

	EV	Fair and Square Party		Do Right Party	
		EV	PV	EV	PV
Voter 27 (1)			1		
Indiana	11	11			
Voter 28 (1)			1		
Massachusetts	11	11			
Voter 29 (1)					1
Georgia	16			16	
Voter 30 (1)					1
Arizona	11			11	
Wyoming	3			3	
Voter 31 (1)			1		
Maryland	10	10			
Voter 32 (1)			1		
Washington	12	12			
Voter 33 (1)			1		
Virginia	13	13			
Voter 34 (1)					1
Tennessee	11			11	
Voter 35 (1)					1
Wisconsin	10			10	
Vermont	3			3	
Voter 36 (1)			1		
Minnesota	10	10			
West Virginia	5	5			
Voter 37 (1)			1		
Missouri	10	10			
Voter 38 (1)			1		
Alabama	9	9			
Alaska	3	3			

	EV	Fair and Square Party		Do Right Party	
		EV	PV	EV	PV
Voter 39 (1)			1		
Arkansas	6	6			
Connecticut	7	7			
Voter 40 (1)			1		
District of Columbia	3	3			
Hawaii	4	4			
Idaho	4	4			
Voter 41 (1)					1
Iowa	6			6	
Kansas	6			6	
Voter 42 (1)					1
Kentucky	8			8	
Maine	4			4	
Voter 43 (1)					1
Louisiana	8			8	
Montana	3			3	
Voter 44 (1)					1
Mississippi	6			6	
Nebraska	5			5	
Voter 45 (1)					1
New Mexico	5			5	
Oklahoma	7			7	
Voter 46 (1)			1		
Oregon	7	7			
Utah	6	6			
Grand Totals	538	260	24	278	22

EV = electoral vote; PV = popular vote

Sample Distribution of Electoral Votes: 240 Students

Below is a random selection of votes per student for a group of 240 students. Students should be given approximately 2 votes each, but the range in this example is approximately 1–6 votes per student. In this example, the Do Right Party wins the election with 309 electoral votes.

	EV	Fair and Square Party		Do Right Party	
		EV	PV	EV	PV
Class 1 (26)					
Voters 1–11 (11)			7		4
Ohio	18	18			
Voters 12–18 (7)			4		3
North Carolina	15	15			
Voter 19 (1)			1		
Delaware	3	3			
Voters 20–24 (5)			2		3
Georgia	16			16	
Voters 25–26 (2)			2		
West Virginia	5	5			
Class 2 (27)					
Voters 1–9 (9)			4		5
Illinois	20			20	
Voter 10 (1)			1		
Hawaii	4	4			
Voter 11 (1)			1		
Montana	3	3			
Voters 12–16 (5)			2		3
Arizona	11			11	
Voters 17–23 (7)			3		4
Virginia	13			13	
Voters 24–26 (3)			1		2
Kentucky	8			8	
Voter 27 (1)			1		
Maine	4	4			
Class 3 (19)					
Voters 1–5 (5)			3		2
Washington	12	12			
Voters 6–8 (3)			1		2
Colorado	9			9	
Voters 9–11 (3)			1		2
Nevada	6			6	
Voter 12 (1)					1
South Dakota	3			3	
Voters 13–15 (3)			2		1
Oregon	7	7			
Voter 16 (1)			1		
Idaho	4	4			
Voters 17–19 (3)			2		1
Kansas	6	6			
Class 4 (27)					
Voters 1–27 (27)			10		17
California	55			55	
Class 5 (25)					
Voters 1–17 (17)			13		4
Texas	38	38			
Voters 18–22 (5)			2		3
Oklahoma	7			7	
Voters 23–25 (3)			2		1
New Mexico	5	5			
Class 6 (25)					
Voters 1–13 (13)			6		7
Florida	29			29	
Voters 14–24 (11)			4		7
Pennsylvania	20			20	
Voter 25 (1)					1
Wyoming	3			3	
Class 7 (23)					
Voters 1–9 (9)			4		5
Michigan	16			16	
Voters 10–12 (3)			2		1
Minnesota	10	10			
Voters 13–15 (3)			2		1
Wisconsin	10	10			
Voters 16–20 (5)			2		3
Indiana	11			11	
Voters 21–23 (3)			2		1
Iowa	6	6			
Class 8 (25)					
Voters 1–7 (7)			3		4
New Jersey	14			14	
Voters 8–20 (13)			7		6
New York	29	29			
Voter 21 (1)			1		
Arkansas	6	6			
Voter 22 (1)					1
North Dakota	3			3	
Voters 23–25 (3)			2		1
South Carolina	9	9			
Class 9 (20)					
Voters 1–7 (7)			3		4
Massachusetts	11			11	
Voters 8–12 (5)			1		4
Missouri	10			10	
Voter 13 (1)			1		
Utah	6	6			
Voters 14–16 (3)			1		2
Connecticut	7			7	
Voter 17 (1)			1		
Vermont	3	3			
Voter 18 (1)			1		
Rhode Island	4	4			
Voter 19 (1)					1
New Hampshire	4	4			
Voter 20 (1)					1
District of Columbia	3			3	
Class 10 (23)					
Voters 1–5 (5)			2		3
Maryland	10			10	
Voters 6–12 (7)			4		3
Tennessee	11	11			
Voters 13–15 (3)			2		1
Louisiana	8	8			
Voters 16–18 (3)			1		2
Alabama	9			9	
Voter 19 (1)			1		
Alaska	3	3			
Voters 20–22 (3)			1		2
Mississippi	6			6	
Voter 23 (1)					1
Nebraska	5			5	
Grand totals	**538**	**229**	**120**	**309**	**120**

EV = electoral vote; PV = popular vote

Allocation of Electoral Votes and Results of the Election

EV	Fair and Square Party		Do Right Party															
	EV	PV	EV	PV														

EV	Fair and Square Party		Do Right Party															
	EV	PV	EV	PV														

EV	Fair and Square Party		Do Right Party															
	EV	PV	EV	PV														

When possible, to avoid a tie, no voting bloc should have an even number of voters. The candidate with a majority of popular votes in a bloc gets the entire electoral votes for all states in that bloc. EV = electoral vote; PV = popular vote

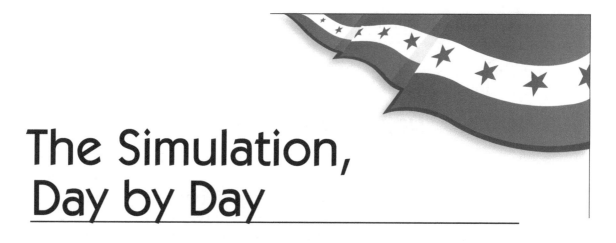

The Simulation, Day by Day

Day 1: Introduction

✓ On Day 1, begin by introducing the procedure for electing the President and Vice President of the United States.

✓ Explain how the popular vote is used to determine the electoral vote and how the President and Vice President are actually elected by the Electoral College.

✓ Show students the map on page 31 and help them understand how the states with larger representation in Congress have more electoral votes.

✓ Explain that citizens must be registered before they can vote. Have all students complete the first two columns of the Voter Registration form (p. 32).

✓ Explain that this simulation does not deal with the state primaries and caucuses. Although in real life this is an essential first step before the parties meet and choose their candidates, it will not be reenacted in class. The simulation will begin with the party conventions.

Day 2: Candidacy Declared

✓ On Day 2, divide students into two groups representing the Do Right party and the Fair and Square party.

✓ Make sure students understand the requirements for holding the offices of President and Vice President.

✓ Each group will meet separately. Any student wishing to run for President will declare his or her candidacy by signing a Declaration of Candidacy statement (p. 26). If working with a large group, you may require the student to receive endorsements from two other students. This requirement may be waived with smaller groups.

✓ Campaigning to become the party's presidential nominee begins.

 DOI: 10.4324/9781003234869-5

Day 3: Party Conventions

- ✓ On Day 3, each party will hold its convention to select presidential and vice presidential candidates and to decide on a platform. At this stage, the students do not need to represent different states.
- ✓ Candidates will give speeches and try to convince members of their party to vote for them. Although they may use the Election Issues handout (pp. 27–30) as a guideline to help them prepare their speeches, there should also be emphasis on their personal qualifications.
- ✓ Students not running for office will select their party's candidate. In this simulation, it is more practical to allow one vote for each student rather than to allow the students to represent states as is done in actual conventions.
- ✓ Election for each party's nominee is held. Should no candidate receive a majority of the votes on the first ballot, hold a run-off between the two candidates who have received the most votes. The losing candidates may instruct their delegates to vote for one of the two remaining candidates, but all delegates are free to vote as they choose. The winning candidate will then select his or her running mate for Vice President.
- ✓ Each party should decide on its platform. It is important that the presidential and vice presidential candidates for each party agree on their stands on important issues.

Day 4: Election Campaign

- ✓ Day 4 begins a new part of the simulation. During the party conventions, students could only vote for candidates in the party to which they were assigned. At this point, the conventions are over and students are no longer delegates. Instead, they will represent the voting public. They *do not* have to vote for the candidate who was elected at the convention in which they took part. They may now vote for either candidate. At this point, students are assigned the state (or states) they will represent. They will now have two identities: One will be the single vote they cast (the popular vote), and they will also represent certain electoral votes.
- ✓ Discuss rules for campaigning. Have students brainstorm a list of ways to present their qualifications and stands on issues to the voters. These can include speeches, posters, buttons, and press releases, among others. Under your direction and following the guidelines that you developed prior to beginning the simulation, the class should decide on the rules for campaigning.

✓ Assign the electoral votes as evenly as possible using the instructions and examples on pages 13–20 as a guide. The three charts on pages 17–19 show samples of how this was done with a class of 15 students, a group of 46 students, and a larger group of 240 students. It also shows the results of the election and how popular votes determine electoral votes. You can use the blank form on page 20 to assign electoral votes.

✓ The Assignment of Electoral College Vote form (p. 33) should be completed and distributed to students. Instead of assigning voting blocs, you can have students draw from a hat for the states they represent. This procedure provides a better chance that students who might not otherwise be motivated will have a greater influence in the process.

✓ Candidates should be aware of which students represent each state. Show this information on a map or give students nameplates with their states on them.

✓ Candidates should begin campaigning to try to persuade other students to vote for them.

Day 5: Speeches

✓ On Day 5, candidates will give their final speeches and try to convince students to vote for them. The presidential and vice presidential candidates for each party should each address different issues of the party's platform in their speeches.

✓ Students may use the Election Issues handout (pp. 27–30) or a list you provide to help them prepare speeches. Explain that the issues listed are very general, and the candidates should explore these ideas in more detail and decide how they feel about each one. They should look up facts that will support their positions. It is possible that opposing candidates may have similar viewpoints or that a viewpoint on an issue may be somewhere between the two extremes. Give candidates a time range for the length of their speeches (e.g., 3–5 minutes). Younger students may require less time.

Day 6: Election Day

✓ On Day 6, students will re-sign the Voter Registration form (p. 32) in the third column and have their signatures verified. Assign one student to be the elections clerk; he or she will be responsible for verifying signatures.

✓ Distribute ballots. In cases where one student represents all of the votes for a voting bloc (either one state or a group of states), you can skip the popular vote and only use the electoral ballots. In cases where several students represent a voting bloc, you will need to distribute a popular ballot to each student and also electoral ballots for each state the voting bloc represents.

✓ Students cast their votes. The popular vote (one vote for each student) and the electoral vote (for the state or states each voting bloc represents) should then be tallied. You can use the Allocation of Electoral Votes and Results of the Election form on page 20 or the Election Vote Tally form on page 36 to record votes.

Day 7: Evaluation

✓ On Day 7, the students will compare the popular and electoral votes each candidate received. Discuss what candidates might do in an actual campaign to try to gain the most electoral votes (e.g., campaign in the most populous states, campaign in the states that are divided).

✓ If this is an actual election year, have students observe how real candidates try to influence voters and which states receive the most attention from each nominee.

Adaptations and Extensions for an Election Year

Adaptations

During an election year, you may not wish to have students participate in the simulation as outlined on pages 21–24, but you may want them to understand the Electoral College process and be able to relate this to the real election as they follow it. In this case, you will not reenact the convention part of the campaign and will not have any student candidates. You will, however, assign the electoral votes as in one of the scenarios described in Apportioning Electoral Votes (pp. 13–20). Ballots should list the names of the actual candidates running for President and Vice President. Have students vote for the actual candidates. Translate their votes to electoral votes and tally the electoral votes to determine the winner. After the election, compare your results to the actual national election tallies. You may also wish to compare your popular vote to that of your community. This method works particularly well with a large group of several classes or an entire school population.

Extensions

✓ As the election heats up, ask students to research each candidate's stand on various issues. Have them make a chart to show the differences (or similarities) among the candidates.

✓ If several classes participate in the election, post a map of the state (or states) a class represents outside the classroom door.

✓ You may wish to have students research their states for information such as the state motto, industries or agricultural products, history, or famous individuals who were born there.

✓ A large chart listing the states, the electoral votes for each, and the school, local, and national popular votes may be posted in a central location.

✓ Have an older class organize a schoolwide election and be responsible for preparing and distributing ballots and tallying the final vote.

DOI: 10.4324/9781003234869-6

DECLARATION OF CANDIDACY

As a member of the _____ party,

I, _____, do hereby declare that I am

a candidate for President of the United States of America.

I certify that I meet the requirements for candidacy as set forth in the Eligibility

Rules for President of the United States of America.

I promise that should I be elected, I will faithfully execute the office of President

of the United States and will, to the best of my ability, preserve, protect, and

defend the Constitution of the United States of America.

_____   _____
Candidate's Signature   Print or Type Name

_____
Date

Endorsed by:

_____   _____

(Endorsements may be optional)

DOI: 10.4324/9781003234869-7

Election Issues

★ ★ Military Appropriations ★ ★

The United States must have the best military forces in the world if we are going to remain a strong nation. Defense of our nation is our country's highest priority, and a large part of the budget should support this function.

Although the military is important, it is more important to work with other nations to maintain peaceful relationships so we don't have to spend a lot of money on military forces. It would be better to spend this money on issues like education and the environment.

★ ★ Health Services ★ ★

We have the best hospitals and health care in the world. Some other countries control health care (socialized medicine), and their citizens do not have the quality of medical care that we do. The government should assure basic medical services only to poor and older citizens. Everyone else should pay for his or her own health services.

Too many people do not have adequate health care. As medical services get more expensive, it is harder for people to pay for doctors and prescriptions. It is up to the government to make sure that everyone receives good, economical medical care.

★ ★ Unemployment ★ ★

There are times when there will be unemployment. It is up to private industry to provide jobs. Government should not get involved in regulating business, providing employment, or setting up training programs.

Businesses do what is best for their profits, not what is best for their employees. Unemployment creates many other social problems, so the government must create jobs or offer incentives to businesses so that everyone who wants a job will have one.

DOI: 10.4324/9781003234869-8

Women's Rights

Because many women have children to care for, they cannot devote as much time and energy to their jobs as men can. It is unfair to expect women to receive the same salary and have the same opportunities as men who do not take time from their jobs for maternity leave or to care for a sick child or relative.

Women contribute important skills to the workforce and should have the same rights and opportunities to advance in their jobs as men. Women should be paid the same as men who hold the same job. We need legislation that will force employers to treat women fairly.

Energy Policy

The United States government should encourage and help pay for solar power and other renewable energy sources. We have to stop our dependence on oil companies. The government should have greater control over these companies and be able to control high prices for gas and oil.

The only way to be truly independent is to end government control on prices or any part of the energy industry. Allow the industry to do what it does best— bring low-cost oil and gas products to everyone—and prices will stay low.

Nuclear Power

We should use other energy sources that are safer than nuclear energy to manufacture electricity. If there were an accident in a nuclear power plant, many people would be killed or suffer long-term health effects. The government should not license any more nuclear power plants and should fund research to develop safer power sources.

Nuclear power plants have been in operation for many years and offer a safe, clean method of providing energy. Other power sources such as coal-burning plants pollute the air. The government should give special consideration and funding to companies that are constructing nuclear power plants.

★　★　Taxes　★　★

The government must have enough income (taxes) to pay for all of its programs. The things the government spends money on are worthwhile projects that pay for services that all (or most) people need. If the government does not have enough money, it takes out loans, and that ends up costing taxpayers a lot more money in the long run.

The government should not levy high taxes on people. If people have money in their pockets, they will spend it, and that will create more jobs and a better economy. The citizens themselves could pay for many of the services currently provided by the government.

★　★　Environment　★　★

Our future as a species depends on our ability to take care of our planet. If we pollute our air and water and cut down all our forests, we will be harming not only humans but also other animals. The government should have regulations that discourage people and companies from ruining the environment.

When we put restraints on companies and force them to clean up pollution, it ends up costing them a lot of money, and they pass this cost on to the consumer. This is bad for the economy. If we just leave companies alone, they will do what is reasonable. Besides, there's not really as much of an environmental problem as some people would have you believe.

★　★　Gun Control　★　★

The right to bear arms was intended for a different time. Guns are most often used to commit crimes. Guns for hunting are okay, but no one needs semi-automatic weapons. By controlling the sale and registration of guns, the government can make sure guns do not get into the hands of people who will use them to harm other people.

The right to carry a gun is guaranteed by the Bill of Rights. This means anyone should be able to own and carry any kind of gun they want. There should be no restrictions or background checks.

★ ★ Free Speech ★ ★ ★

People should be able to say anything they want at any time and via any media. We are guaranteed freedom of speech in the Bill of Rights and that means that there should be no restrictions on what you say.

You are free to speak, but there have to be some limitations on language that is hateful, offensive, or objectionable to other people.

★ ★ Education ★ ★

Education is a function of the states, and the federal government should not get involved. It is up to each state to fund its schools and set standards for its students. If some states have more money to give to schools and, hence, their students get a better education, that's not a big problem.

It is important that all school children in the country have a good education. There should be national educational standards for all students, and children should be tested each year to make sure they are meeting these standards. The federal government should give poorer schools money so they can provide an education equal to the richer schools.

★ ★ Federal Lands ★ ★

The role of the federal government should be to preserve land and make it available for all people to enjoy, both now and in the future. This should be done through national parks, forests, and wilderness areas. Our environment is very fragile, and the lands that the government owns are in areas that are easily spoiled. The government should protect these areas and make sure people don't damage or exploit them.

The federal government already owns too much land. It should not acquire any additional land. When it owns land that could be used for other things (e.g., mining, oil exploration, logging, grazing), it should rent the land to private companies and let them use the resources. It makes no sense to leave these resources untapped when they could be used to provide income and energy.

Electoral Votes Map

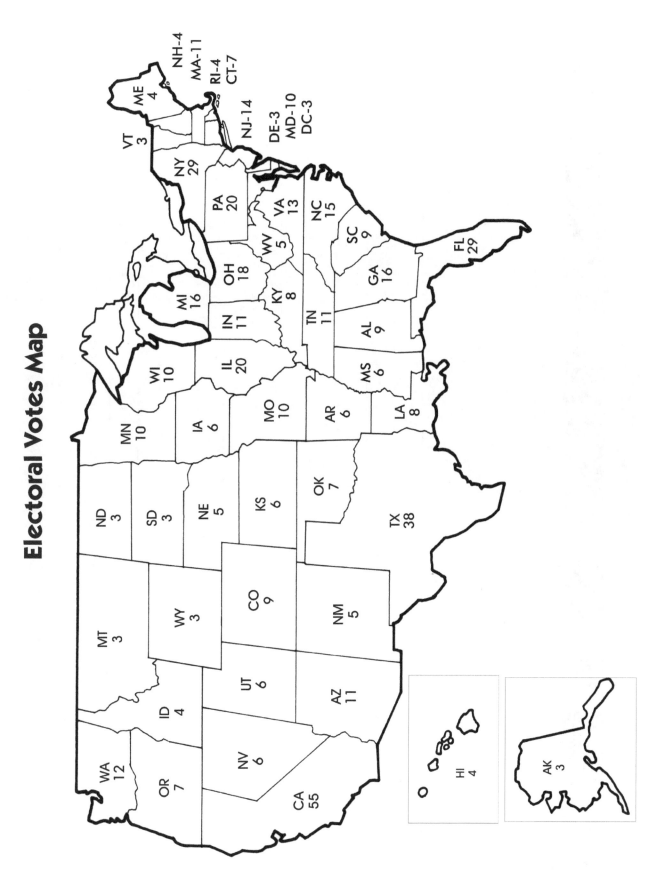

DOI: 10.4324/9781003234869-9

Voter Registration

Voter's Name (Printed)	Voter's Signature (At time of registration)	Voter's Signature (On Election Day)	Signature Verified

To Register: Have the voter print his or her name in the first column and write his or her signature in the second column.

To Vote: On Election Day, have the voter sign in the third column next to his or her name. The two signatures will be compared and verified by an elections clerk who will initial the last column.

DOI: 10.4324/9781003234869-10

ASSIGNMENT OF
ELECTORAL COLLEGE VOTE

★ ★ ★ ★

U.S. PRESIDENTIAL ELECTION

★ ★ ★

Name: _____
(Name of student or class)

You have been assigned the following states and electoral votes:

State	Votes
_____	_____
_____	_____
_____	_____
_____	_____
_____	_____

ASSIGNMENT OF
ELECTORAL COLLEGE VOTE

★ ★ ★ ★

U.S. PRESIDENTIAL ELECTION

★ ★ ★

Name: _____
(Name of student or class)

You have been assigned the following states and electoral votes:

State	Votes
_____	_____
_____	_____
_____	_____
_____	_____
_____	_____

DOI: 10.4324/9781003234869-11

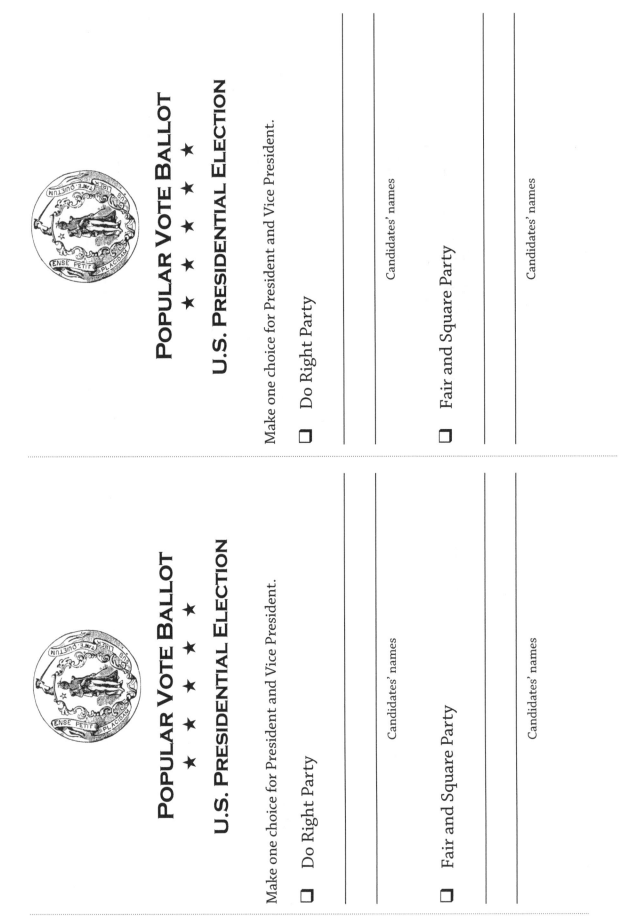

POPULAR VOTE BALLOT
★ ★ ★ ★ ★

U.S. PRESIDENTIAL ELECTION

Make one choice for President and Vice President.

☐ Do Right Party

_____
Candidates' names

☐ Fair and Square Party

_____
Candidates' names

POPULAR VOTE BALLOT
★ ★ ★ ★ ★

U.S. PRESIDENTIAL ELECTION

Make one choice for President and Vice President.

☐ Do Right Party

_____
Candidates' names

☐ Fair and Square Party

_____
Candidates' names

DOI: 10.4324/9781003234869-12

ELECTORAL VOTE BALLOT ★ ★ ★ ★ ★
U.S. PRESIDENTIAL ELECTION

State: _____

Votes: _____

Make one choice for President and Vice President.

☐ Do Right Party

_____
Candidates' names

☐ Fair and Square Party

_____
Candidates' names

ELECTORAL VOTE BALLOT ★ ★ ★ ★ ★
U.S. PRESIDENTIAL ELECTION

State: _____

Votes: _____

Make one choice for President and Vice President.

☐ Do Right Party

_____
Candidates' names

☐ Fair and Square Party

_____
Candidates' names

Election Vote Tally

States	Electoral Votes	Fair and Square Party		Do Right Party	
		Popular Votes	Electoral Votes	Popular Votes	Electoral Votes
Alabama	9				
Alaska	3				
Arizona	11				
Arkansas	6				
California	55				
Colorado	9				
Connecticut	7				
Delaware	3				
District of Columbia	3				
Florida	29				
Georgia	16				
Hawaii	4				
Idaho	4				
Illinois	20				
Indiana	11				
Iowa	6				
Kansas	6				
Kentucky	8				
Louisiana	8				
Maine	4				
Maryland	10				
Massachusetts	11				
Michigan	16				
Minnesota	10				
Mississippi	6				
Missouri	10				
Montana	3				

States	Electoral Votes	Fair and Square Party		Do Right Party	
		Popular Votes	Electoral Votes	Popular Votes	Electoral Votes
Nebraska	5				
Nevada	6				
New Hampshire	4				
New Jersey	14				
New Mexico	5				
New York	29				
North Carolina	15				
North Dakota	3				
Ohio	18				
Oklahoma	7				
Oregon	7				
Pennsylvania	20				
Rhode Island	4				
South Carolina	9				
South Dakota	3				
Tennessee	11				
Texas	38				
Utah	6				
Vermont	3				
Virginia	13				
Washington	12				
West Virginia	5				
Wisconsin	10				
Wyoming	3				
Total (both columns)	538				

DOI: 10.4324/9781003234869-14

Election Vote Tally
State Votes for an Election Year

States	Electoral Votes	Democrat	Republican	Third Party
Alabama	9			
Alaska	3			
Arizona	11			
Arkansas	6			
California	55			
Colorado	9			
Connecticut	7			
Delaware	3			
District of Columbia	3			
Florida	29			
Georgia	16			
Hawaii	4			
Idaho	4			
Illinois	20			
Indiana	11			
Iowa	6			
Kansas	6			
Kentucky	8			
Louisiana	8			
Maine	4			
Maryland	10			
Massachusetts	11			
Michigan	16			
Minnesota	10			
Mississippi	6			
Missouri	10			

States	Electoral Votes	Democrat	Republican	Third Party
Montana	3			
Nebraska	5			
Nevada	6			
New Hampshire	4			
New Jersey	14			
New Mexico	5			
New York	29			
North Carolina	15			
North Dakota	3			
Ohio	18			
Oklahoma	7			
Oregon	7			
Pennsylvania	20			
Rhode Island	4			
South Carolina	9			
South Dakota	3			
Tennessee	11			
Texas	38			
Utah	6			
Vermont	3			
Virginia	13			
Washington	12			
West Virginia	5			
Wisconsin	10			
Wyoming	3			
Vote Totals				

DOI: 10.4324/9781003234869-15

Permission is granted to photocopy or reproduce this page for single classroom use only.

Electing Our President Simulation Overview

Electing the U.S. President is an important task undertaken by voters every 4 years. During an election year, you'll hear many advertisements on television and radio supporting various candidates who are running for election. You may notice mail coming to your house that shares information about certain politicians and why you should vote for them. You may become more interested in all of the political messages, as you will be participating in a simulation of the election process.

You are going to be an elector for a particular state (or states). You realize that this is a very important position. It is the link between the popular votes (the vote that takes place in November when all registered voters can vote for the candidates of their choice) and the selection of a President and Vice President. You represent one party, either the Fair and Square Party or the Do Right Party. Once the popular vote has taken place, if your party wins the majority of the popular votes, you will be able to cast your elector votes for your party's candidate. You hope your party's candidate wins at the polls in November because then you can exercise your duties as an elector.

As you and your classmates work through this simulation, you will see how a real election works. From the very beginning, when several people decide that they want to run for President, through the campaigning and election, to the final vote of the electors, you will take an active part in the election process. You will get the opportunity to be an elector that represents one or more states. As the elector from this state (or states), you will cast your vote for your party's candidate if this candidate won the popular vote. You will be the official link between the popular vote (the total of all of the votes cast at polling places throughout your state) and who is actually elected President and Vice President. This will help you understand our political system better and be a more informed voter when you are old enough to cast your vote in a real election.

DOI: 10.4324/9781003234869-16

★ The Election Process ★

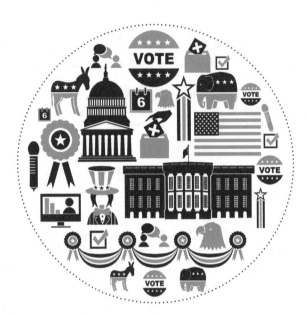

The Constitution of the United States provides a unique method of electing our President and Vice President. In most elections, the candidate receiving the most votes is the winner; however, in our presidential elections, the Electoral College makes the final decision. Does this mean that the vote cast by each citizen does not count? Not at all. Here is the way our system works.

Choosing a Candidate

Presidential elections are held every 4 years in November. Primary elections or caucuses are held in states during the spring (January to June) prior to the November election. During the primary elections and caucuses, voters select from a large number of candidates running in their party's election. Depending on the state, voters may be required to be a registered member of a party to vote in the primary. There are several political parties in the United States, including the Green Party, Reform Party, and Libertarian Party, as well as the two largest, the Republican and Democratic parties. Although candidates from all parties are on the ballots for both the general election, and all parties hold conventions, the two largest parties usually get most of the attention.

DOI: 10.4324/9781003234869-17

During the summer before the election, the political parties hold their national conventions. At these conventions, party delegates (as outlined in each party's rules) vote until one candidate has received the majority of the votes. If no candidate is selected on the first ballot, the delegates will continue to vote until someone receives at least half of the total delegate vote. In recent history, there has typically been a single front-runner who has already received the majority of the party's delegates and so only one vote has been needed.

Thus, each party will nominate a presidential candidate who will compete with all of the other parties' candidates in the national election in November. Once the presidential candidate is selected, he or she chooses someone who will be a vice presidential running mate. The two together are sometimes referred to as the "presidential ticket." There are typically other candidates in the running besides the Republican and Democratic nominees, but the nominee from one of the two largest parties almost always wins.

Campaigning

Between the end of the national conventions and Election Day, there is intense campaigning by the presidential and vice presidential candidates. This campaigning might take the form of advertisements on TV, on the radio, or in the newspapers; personal appearances throughout the country; special mailings; televised debates; and telemarketing. In each instance, candidates share their viewpoints on certain issues and each tries to convince the voters that he or she would be the best individual to fill the role of President or Vice President.

The Popular Vote

On Election Day, which is the first Tuesday after the first Monday in November, voters go to the polls to cast their votes for the candidates of their choice. At this time, there might also be an election for local or state officials and for members of the U.S. House of Representatives and the U.S. Senate. There may also be propositions on

the ballot asking the voters to decide on a particular issue such as whether or not the state should require people to show a photo ID when voting.

The votes cast by individual voters are called the popular vote. This is the first step in electing the President; however, the president is not actually chosen by popular vote. The candidate who receives the most votes in a state wins all of the electoral votes for the state (except in Maine and Nebraska, in which the votes are allocated proportionally). The elector votes are what actually determine who will be President.

To determine the number of electoral votes, the number of members the state has in the U.S. House of Representatives is added to the two senators that each state has in the U.S. Senate. For example:

The state of Florida has the following:
Representatives: 27
Senators: 2
Total electoral votes: 29

When Americans vote for a President and Vice President, they are really voting for a slate of electors who pledge to vote for their candidates. In all, there are 538 electoral votes, and a majority (more than half), or 270 votes, is needed to elect a President and Vice President. It is possible to win the popular vote and lose the election. This has happened three times in our history.

The Electoral College

The victorious presidential and vice presidential nominees in each state win the state's entire electoral vote no matter how small their margin of victory. After the popular vote is counted in each state, the candidate receiving the most votes is awarded all of that state's electoral votes. Maine and Nebraska are the only states that do not have a winner-take-all way to allocate electoral votes. For example:

If 1,509,734 of the voters in the state of Minnesota voted for Willy Wannabe of the Republican party and 1,509,101 voters cast their votes for Elmer Electme of the Democratic party, the Republican candidate would get all of Minnesota's electoral votes and the Democratic candidate would get none.

In December, the electors from the party whose candidates have received the most popular votes meet in their state capitals and cast their ballots for their state's candidates. The candidates who receive the majority of the electoral votes win the office of President and Vice President. For example:

The Republican candidate wins 265 electoral votes.
The Democratic candidate wins 270 electoral votes.
The Libertarian candidate wins 3 electoral votes.
The winner would be the Democratic candidate.

Steps to the Presidency

1 **Declaration:** Candidates declare their intention to run for President.

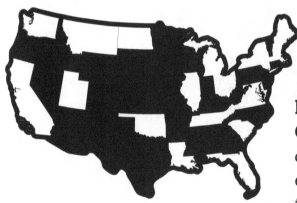

2 **Primary Elections and Caucuses:** Candidates compete in the primary elections and caucuses throughout the states.

3 **Conventions:** The parties hold their conventions to select the party's candidates and decide on its platform.

DOI: 10.4324/9781003234869-18

4

Campaigns: The presidential and vice presidential candidates for each party campaign in all states.

5

Popular Vote: The election is held in November, and all registered voters cast their ballots for their favorite presidential candidate. The person who wins the popular votes wins all of the elector votes for that state (except for Maine and Nebraska).

6

Electoral Vote: The electors from the winning party of each state meet and cast their votes for their party's choice for President and Vice President.

7

Winner Declared: The person with a majority of at least 270 electoral votes becomes President. His or her running mate becomes Vice President.

Appendix
The U.S. Constitution, Article II and Amendment XII

Article II
Section 1

The executive Power shall be vested in a President of the United States of America. He shall hold his Office during the Term of four Years, and, together with the Vice President, chosen for the same Term, be elected, as follows:

Each State shall appoint, in such Manner as the Legislature thereof may direct, a Number of Electors, equal to the whole Number of Senators and Representatives to which the State may be entitled in the Congress: but no Senator or Representative, or Person holding an Office of Trust or Profit under the United States, shall be appointed an Elector.

[*The clause included in the original Constitution has been eliminated here because it was superseded by the Twelfth Amendment.*]

The Congress may determine the Time of chusing [*sic*] the Electors, and the Day on which they shall give their Votes; which Day shall be the same throughout the United States.

No Person except a natural born Citizen, or a Citizen of the United States, at the time of the Adoption of this Constitution, shall be eligible to the Office of President; neither shall any Person be eligible to that Office who shall not have attained to the Age of thirty five Years, and been fourteen Years a Resident within the United States.

Note: Additional parts of this section define the rules for succession, oath of office, and compensation for the President.

Amendment XII (Passed by Congress Dec. 9, 1803; ratified June 15, 1804)

The Electors shall meet in their respective states and vote by ballot for President and Vice-President, one of whom, at least, shall not be an inhabitant of the same state with themselves; they shall name in their ballots the

person voted for as President, and in distinct ballots the person voted for as Vice-President, and they shall make distinct lists of all persons voted for as President, and of all persons voted for as Vice-President, and of the number of votes for each, which lists they shall sign and certify, and transmit sealed to the seat of the government of the United States, directed to the President of the Senate; -- the President of the Senate shall, in the presence of the Senate and House of Representatives, open all the certificates and the votes shall then be counted; -- The person having the greatest number of votes for President, shall be the President, if such number be a majority of the whole number of Electors appointed; and if no person have such majority, then from the persons having the highest numbers not exceeding three on the list of those voted for as President, the House of Representatives shall choose immediately, by ballot, the President. But in choosing the President, the votes shall be taken by states, the representation from each state having one vote; a quorum for this purpose shall consist of a member or members from two-thirds of the states, and a majority of all the states shall be necessary to a choice.

[*A clause is included here in the original Constitution providing for the Vice President to act as President if the House did not choose the President in a timely fashion. This was superseded by Section 3 of Amendment XX.*]

The person having the greatest number of votes as Vice-President, shall be the Vice-President, if such number be a majority of the whole number of Electors appointed, and if no person have a majority, then from the two highest numbers on the list, the Senate shall choose the Vice-President; a quorum for the purpose shall consist of two-thirds of the whole number of Senators, and a majority of the whole number shall be necessary to a choice. But no person constitutionally ineligible to the office of President shall be eligible to that of Vice-President of the United States.

These are transcriptions of Article II and the Twelfth Amendment to the U.S. Constitution in their original forms.

About the Author

Betty M. See returned to college after the youngest of her four children entered kindergarten. She earned her bachelor's degree in English and master's degree in reading. She has had a varied teaching career. She taught seventh- and eighth-grade language arts, was a middle school classroom teacher, teaching all subject areas, and for 10 years worked with gifted students in grades 3–8 in Little Falls, NJ.

At each of these levels, she often used simulation activities to help students become involved in the learning process. In 1992, she received an A+ for Kids Teacher Network Award for a simulation activity, *Celebrating Our Heritage*.

Mock trials were among the favorite activities of her students. Finding little suitable prepared material, she wrote trials using characters familiar to the students. These trials were the basis for her successful first book, *Jury Trials in the Classroom*. Her second book, *Electing the President*, started as a simulation to help her fourth-grade social studies students understand the election process and was later adapted for gifted students, resulting in a schoolwide project for an actual presidential election. Responses from classroom teachers were positive, stating that this simulation helped students understand the Electoral College concept and how the President was elected. Her most recent book, *More Jury Trials in the Classroom* was published in 2007. As with the first book, she created trials in which the participants are familiar, adding an element of humor to further pique the interest of students.

See has retired from the classroom, but has never given up her love of teaching and writing. She and her husband, Bob, retired to Florida and live at the Leeward Air Ranch, where he flies his Piper Archer, and she is editor of the community newsletter. In addition to editing, she regularly submits humorous columns about aviation and life in general.